Remembrance Day

Kay Barnham

Explore the world with **Popcorn** – your complete first non-fiction library.

Look out for more titles in the **Popcorn** range. All books have the same format of simple text and striking images. Text is carefully matched to the pictures to help readers to identify and understand key vocabulary.
www.waylandbooks.co.uk/popcorn

First published in 2009 by Wayland

This paperback edition published in 2010 and 2011 by Wayland

Copyright © Wayland 2009

Wayland
Hachette Children's Books
338 Euston Road
London NW1 3BH

Wayland Australia
Level 17/207 Kent Street
Sydney NSW 2000

Editor: Katie Powell
Designer: Phipps Design

British Library Cataloguing in Publication Data
 Barnham, Kay
    Remembrance Day. - (Popcorn. History corner)
    1. Armistice Day - Juvenile literature
    2. Remembrance Sunday - Juvenile literature
    I. Title
    940.4'39

ISBN: 978 0 7502 6420 4

Printed and bound in China

Wayland is a division of Hachette Children's Books, an Hachette UK Company.
www.hachette.co.uk

Photographs:
AFP/Getty Images: 18, Bettmann/Corbis: 10, Paul Grover/Rex Features: 15, David Hancock/Alamy: 19, Julian Herbert/Rex Features: Cover, 4-5, National Army Museum, London/Bridgeman Art Library, London: title page, 6, OJPHOTOS/Alamy: 20, 23, Panoramic Images/Getty Images: 16-17, Steve Parsons/PA Archive/PA Photos: 14, Martin Phelps/Alamy: 13, Popperfoto/Getty Images: 2, 7, 9, 11, Print Collector/HIP/TopFoto.co.uk: 8, Chris Radburn/PA Archive/PA Photos: 12, Bob Watkins/Photofusion: 21

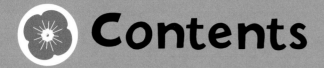 # Contents

A day to remember

Every year in November, there is a special day called Remembrance Day. It takes place on 11th November.

People lay wreaths at war memorials on Remembrance Day.

On Remembrance Day, people around
the world remember those who have
died in wars.

The First World War

In 1914, the First World War began. It was
a long and bloody war that lasted four years.
Many countries and millions of soldiers took part.

At the Battle of the Somme, 20,000 soldiers died
on the first day of fighting.

Soldiers fought on huge battlefields.
When they weren't fighting, they lived
in cold, muddy trenches.

The trenches were filled with rats.
Many soldiers caught awful diseases.

The end of the war

The First World War ended at the 11th hour on the 11th day of the 11th month in 1918. The agreement that ended the war was called the Armistice.

Everyone celebrated in the streets at the end of the war.

King George V decided that
11th November should be called
Armistice Day. On this day,
everyone would remember
those who died in the war.

By the end of
the First World
War, more than
8 million soldiers
had died.

The Second World War

In 1939, the Second World War broke out. It was the biggest war in history. Millions of soldiers died during fighting. Millions more civilians were killed during air raids.

The war was fought on land, at sea and in the air.

After the war ended in 1945, Armistice Day became known as Remembrance Day. It was now a day to remember the dead from both world wars.

Air-raid wardens, police officers, doctors and nurses risked their lives to save others during the war.

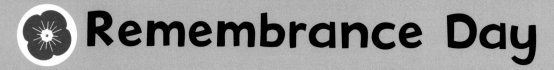 # Remembrance Day

At exactly 11am on Remembrance Day, people are quiet for two minutes to remember those who have died in wars.

In some countries, there are parades in towns and cities. Ceremonies and church services are held around the world.

 Remembrance Sunday

In Britain, there is a two-minute silence on Remembrance Sunday. This is the nearest Sunday to 11th November.

Both old and young remember those who have died.

On this day, there are ceremonies at war memorials around the country. Members of the royal family lay wreaths at The Cenotaph in London.

Here Prince William lays a wreath on Remembrance Sunday.

How people are remembered

All around the world, there are memorials to remind us of people who have died in wars and conflicts.

Some memorials are crosses and others are statues. But there are also sundials, benches and plaques that list the names of people who died.

This huge wall in Washington DC, USA, lists the names of soldiers who died in the Vietnam War (1959–1975).

Remembering around the world

On Remembrance Day, people in many countries remember those who fought, and those who died, in recent wars and wars from long ago.

In 2007, soldiers fighting in Afghanistan held a Remembrance Day service.

In America, war dead are also remembered on Memorial Day in May. In Australia and New Zealand people remember their war dead on 25th April, as well as 11th November.

These women in Australia remember their fathers, who died during the Second World War.

 # Poppies

After the First World War, poppies were among the only plants to grow on the battlefields in France.

Today, many people wear poppies on Remembrance Day. The red flowers show that they remember those who have died in all wars.

Money collected from the sale of poppies helps to support soldiers.

Paint a 'poppy field'

Make your own 'poppy field' painting to remember those who have died in wars and conflicts.

You will need:

• a plastic drink bottle
• a long piece of string
• some cling film
• 1 piece of A4 paper
• 2 paintbrushes
• green, red and black poster paints
• PVA glue

1. Paint thin lines of glue in circles around the bottle. Wind the string round the bottle, sticking it to the glue. Leave it to dry.

2. Using your other paintbrush, brush green paint on to a big piece of cling film.

3. Roll the bottle over the paint and then roll it over the paper. Repeat this until you have a grassy field.

4. When the green paint is dry, paint red poppies in your field. Don't forget to add black centres to your poppies!

A First World War poem

John McCrae was a surgeon in the Canadian Army in the First World War. He wrote this poem in 1915, while he was serving on the battlefields in France.

In Flanders Fields *by John McCrae*

In Flanders fields the poppies blow
Between the crosses, row on row,
That mark our place; and in the sky
The larks, still bravely singing, fly
Scarce heard amid the guns below.

We are the dead. Short days ago
We lived, felt dawn, saw sunset glow,
Loved, and were loved, and now we lie
In Flanders fields.

Take up our quarrel with the foe:
To you from failing hands we throw
The torch; be yours to hold it high.
If ye break faith with us who die
We shall not sleep, though poppies grow
In Flanders fields.

Glossary

air raid
when an aircraft flies somewhere so that it can drop bombs

air raid warden
a person who directs others to shelters during an air raid

Canada
a large country in North America

Cenotaph
a war memorial to remember the dead

ceremony
an important and serious service

civilian
a person who is not part of the armed services

conflict
a long struggle between armies

granite
a very hard type of rock

memorial
a structure or statue that is built in memory of a person or event

remembrance
the act of remembering

surgeon
a doctor in the army

trench
a long, narrow hole dug in the ground

wreath
a ring of leaves or flowers

Index